Hand-Knotting Made Easy Volume

12 More Knotted Jewelry Projects to Make with the Easy Knotter

By
Reenie Oliveto

Copyright © 2019 Designs by Reenie

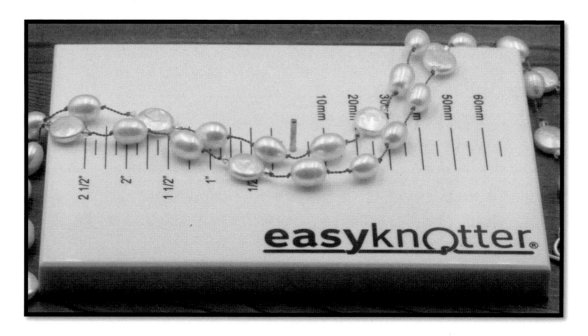

Table of Contents

Introduction

Welcome to *Hand-Knotting Made Easy Volume 2*! Thank you so much to everyone who purchased the first book. I hope you enjoyed it! I'd also like to thank everyone who has supported my business over the years. It's been a thrill traveling the country to teach and vend at bead trade shows.

Your continued support gave me this incredible opportunity to be a guest on Jewelry Television, *Jewel School* back in 2011 with the Easy Knotter. What a day that was. We sold out in minutes. I was able to get another shipment of Easy Knotters for the show and that sold out in minutes. What a feeling. I am humbled by all of this. After the show a group of people came down to congratulate us for a terrific show. I had no idea who they were but I was told later on that one of them was the CEO of the company. This is a day I will always remember. I now appear on *Jewel School* a few times a year. I could not have done this without all of you. And I thank you from the bottom of my heart. Trust me, if you like making beaded jewelry, watch *Jewel School* on Jewelry Television. It's filled with helpful tips, beads and products.

Finally, I'd like to personally thank Christiane Ross. Christiane was incredibly supportive, always ensuring I had everything I wanted and needed for my appearances on *Jewel School*. She truly is a wonderful friend to me. Christiane has now started her own business, OctopusDo, which I encourage you to look into.

Thanks again to everyone! All the encouragement has meant so much. I hope you enjoy this book. Let the designs here inspire you to come up with your own!

Best,
Maureen "Reenie" Oliveto

Easy Knotter Instructions

In this book my instructions are geared towards using the Easy Knotter. Although you can technically make these projects without the Easy Knotter, you can make them much more easily and quickly with this tool. The directions below explain, step-by-step, how to use the Easy Knotter. You can refer to these when working on the projects in this book.

The Easy Knotter is for right-handed and left-handed people. I am right-handed, so I will be using the right side of the Easy Knotter. Use whichever side is best for you.

STEP 1 – Create the loop for the knot and bring your cord through the loop

STEP 2 – Place the loop on the post – ALWAYS HAVE THE LOOP FACING YOU.

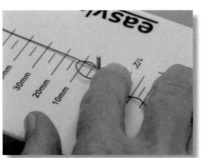

STEP 3 – To close up the loop on the post, I put my index finger up to the post while pressing down lightly on the loop of the cord while pulling the cord with my opposite hand to close up the loop around the post.

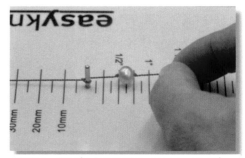

STEP 4 – For the instructions we are using the ½" measurement. In the future, use whichever measurement is appropriate for your project. Pull the cord until your previous knot is at the ½" measurement.

STEP 5 – With your index finger and thumb, lift the knot off the post and give a tug on the cord in your opposite hand while holding the knot. This will tighten the knot. Do not let go of the knot until you have tugged on the cord.

STEP 6 – Bring a bead down to the knot you just created. We want a knot on the other side of the bead.

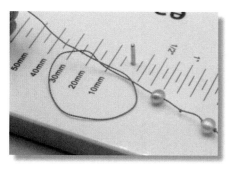

STEP 7 – Create a loop for the knot. Bring the bead and cord through the loop.

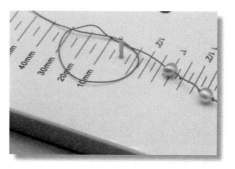

STEP 8 – Place the loop, facing you, on the post. Close up the loop of the knot (Step 3). Pull until the bead is right up to the post. Don't be afraid to pull tight.

STEP 8 CONTINUED - Let the bead go wherever it wants to go – there will be gaps by the bead and post – do not try to close the gaps and do not bring the bead back to the measurement line.

To get the knot off the post and get the knot close to the bead, there are a couple of different methods. Choose whichever method is best for you.

METHOD #1 – *This is the easier method. I would suggest using this method first, then go on to the second method after you have mastered this method.*

STEP 9 – After step 8, bring down the next bead and hold the bead in one hand and the cord in the other hand. When you're about 2" from the knot, gently raise both hands to get the knot off the post and let the knot and bead rest on the board.

STEP 10 – While holding the cord in one hand and the bead in the other hand – in one quick step – push the bead that is in your hand to the knot while pulling on the cord with your opposite hand. The bead will push the knot close to the bead.

STEP 10 CONTINUED - Repeat this process until your project is complete.

METHOD #2 – This method takes a little practice, but once you have mastered it, you will love it. Most important steps to this method is that you need to pull tight on the cord to get that bead up to the post. Once you get hold of the bead and knot, do not move your fingers or thumb. Lift the knot off the post and then tug on the cord making sure you do not move your fingers or thumb.

STEP 9 – After completing Step 8, keep the cord taut, grip the bead with your index finger and your thumb (the bead will be between your index finger and thumb). Place your thumb on the knot and cord. Like a little tripod.

STEP 9 CONTINUED - Give it a good pinch. Make sure you have a good grip of the bead and cord. Once you get a good pinch of the bead and cord, let go of the cord in your other hand. You don't want to tug on the cord while lifting the knot off the post, it will move the knot and the knot will not be close to the bead.

STEP 10 - Lift the knot off the post – most important – do not move your fingers or thumb while lifting the knot off the post. Make sure you pull the knot straight off – no tilting. Grab hold of the cord with your free hand and give a tug on the cord away from the bead. Again, make sure you do not move your fingers or thumb until after you tug on the cord. If you move your fingers or thumb, the knot will not come close to the bead. Repeat this process until your project is completed.

FINISHING YOUR PROJECT – To end the project, after the last knot, bring either the crimping end cap, clam shell or crimp bead to the knot. Using the instructions on how to start the project, you will do the same ending the project. Trim the excess cord, attach a clasp of our choice and enjoy!!

Things to remember while knotting with the Easy Knotter – Always have the loop towards you – When using Method #1 and you have a set of beads (crystal, bead, crystal) and need to take the knot off the post, what you would do, instead of just using the next crystal as your anchor bead, you would use the crystal and bead and then push them to the knot to tighten up the knot. This step makes it easier to close up the knot.

THE EASY KNOTTER IS NOT A TOY AND ADULT SUPERVISION IS NEEDED.

Let's talk about starting and stopping a necklace

I like to use crimping end caps. It gives a nice finished look. The crimping end cap has a closed loop at the top of the crimp so you can easily add your clasp. You would use a 0.8mm inside diameter crimping end caps.

Start with a knot at the end of the cord. Bring the crimping end cap to the knot. Create a knot approximately one inch from the first knot with the crimping end cap floating between the knots. If you like, you can add glue to the cord above the second knot. It's for extra security. Do not get the glue on the other side of the knot, it will discolor the cord.

Bring the crimping end cap to the second knot and crimp using chain nose pliers. Crimp on one side and then crimp again on the other side of the crimping end cap. Don't crimp too hard. You may break the crimping end cap. Give a good tug on the end cap, making sure it is secure.

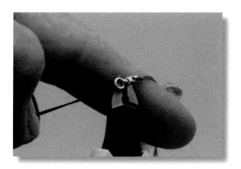

Once the crimping end cap is secure, trim the excess cord.

You can also use a crimp bead. What you would do is tie a knot at the end of the cord. Bring down the crimp bead about one inch from the knot. Next, bring down one closed jump ring.

With the needle, bring the needle back through the crimp bead, making sure you have secured the closed jump ring.

Using the bottom part of the crimping pliers, crimp the crimp bead up to the closed jump ring.

Using the top part of the crimping pliers, crimp the crimp bead closed.

Trim the excess cord.

You can either leave the crimp bead as it is, or you can attach a crimp cover. Crimp covers gives it a more finished look.

With the top part of your crimping pliers, pick up the crimp cover.

Capture the crimp bead within the crimp cover and gently close the crimp cover.

You can also start and stop your project with a clam shell. Start by tying a knot at the end of the cord. Bring the clam shell down to the knot. Add a little bit of glue to the knot. Once the glue dries, trim the excess cord. Attach your clasp to the clam shell and close the clam shell.

I also have projects in the book that do not need any findings. These are quite fun.

Let's talk about cord

My favorite cord is the Griffin nylon or Griffin silk cord. It comes in a variety of colors and sizes. I use mostly size 4 and size 6 for my projects. I use size 4 for my smaller beads and size 6 for larger beads. The Griffin nylon cord is stronger than the Griffin silk cord and it does not stretch. The best part of the cord is that it comes with a needle attached, which makes it very easy to string your beads on the cord.

The package comes with approximately 6 ½ feet of cord. Once you unravel the cord there will be kinks. I use my flat iron (same flat iron that I would use on my hair) to get the kinks out. It works perfectly.

If you want to stretch the cord before knotting, you can clip it on a hanger and have the hanger high enough so you can weigh it down with a 2 lb. weight. You can either put a little tape on the cord and attach it to the weight, or tie a loose knot. Let it hang for a day or two. Or, you can just take the cord and pull the cord every two inches. I usually don't stretch my cord. I like to just flat iron it and go.

With the Easy Knotter, you can use any cord you like, as long as it can hold a knot. Some options besides the silk and nylon are leather, suede, waxed linen, metallic cord, etc.

There are many different sizes of cord. Griffin sizes range from size 0, which is 0.30mm. It's a very thin cord. Griffin goes up to size 16, which is 1.05mm which is a very thick cord.

Silk cord comes in letter sizes. Size A is a very thin cord. 0.1778mm. Silk cord goes up to size FFF which is 0.4191mm. The size FFF is almost equivalent to size 2 in the Griffin cord. When I use size FFF in knotting, I usually double the cord because of how thin it is.

I use the Griffin cord though out my book. If you are not using Griffin cord and need to know how much cord to use, what you would do is use 2.5 times the amount of the project. If your project is 20 inches, you would need 50 inches of cord.

If you are using cord that does not have a needle attached, I found this really great glue (Henrietta's Gum Arabic Beading Glue) that makes a great needle. I just dap a little bit of glue on my fingertips and take approximately 2" at the end of the cord and smooth out the glue. Wait for it to dry and then cut the cord on an angle. Some cords may need to be glued twice. Or, you can simply use a collapsible eye needle, size fine.

KNOTTING TIP: If the bead goes over the knot, you will need to either use a thicker cord, or you can put crystals or seed beads on each side of the bead. That will hold the bead in place. I love using the crystals!!

Let's talk about wire wrapping

Take your headpin and place the beads that you want on it. With your round-nose pliers, bring it to the bead on the headpin. With your index finger at the top of the round-nose pliers, push the head pin to a 90-degree angle.

Take your round-nose pliers and place it at the corner of the 90-degree angle.

With your index finger at the top of the round-nose pliers, push the head pin to a 180-degree angle.

To make the loop of the wire wrap, take your thumb and push the head pin to the bottom of the round-nose pliers.

You can maneuver the round-nose pliers to get a nice round loop.

At this point, when you want to attach something to the wire wrapping, what you need to do is after you got the loop started, open the loop up and take whatever you need to attach and place it in the loop of the wire wrap.

To finish the wire wrapping (with or without an attachment to the loop) take your chain-nose pliers, grab the end of the head pin and start wrapping, starting at the bottom of the loop and working your way down to the bead, with your round-nose pliers in the loop of the wire wrap.

With your cutters, trim the excess wire.

Take your chain-nose pliers and push the wire you just cut into the wire wrap so no wire is showing.

A Note on Materials

Each set of instructions in this book includes a list of materials you'll need to complete the project. That said, it won't always be possible for you to find the exact same beads I used.

That's just all the more reason to get creative! If you're comfortable with doing so, I highly recommend substituting some of the beads I used with your own selections. For instance, maybe you like the overall pattern of one project, but would rather use beads of a different color. Or, perhaps, you'd prefer using beads of a slightly different shape.

That's fine! Again, one of the great benefits of using the Easy Knotter is the chance to try new designs and explore your own creativity. While I recommend sticking to the basic patterns, especially if you're a beginner, I also want you to bring your own personal touch to each project. You can even share your pictures with me through the Designs by Reenie Facebook page. I would love to see what you come up with!

PROJECT 1: MINIMALIST NECKLACE – 18"

SUPPLIES NEEDED   -   Griffin Silk Cord, Size 5, Beige
7 – 3mm round faceted lapis beads
2 – 3mm Swarovski Bicone Crystals
2 – gold plated metal seed beads, size 15
2 – 2x3mm crimp beads
2 – 3mm crimp covers
1 – closed 5mm jump ring
1 – closed 5mm spring ring
1 – ruler

I love all delicate beads. Being a guest on Jewelry Television, Jewel School is the best! I get to see and touch what is going to be shown during the show. My eyes went directly to the 3mm strands. So many different gems and all beautiful!! Had to have them. They are now safely in my possession and the faceted lapis from one of the 3mm strands is what I used for this necklace. The simple design is one of my favorites. It can be worn with anything and you can use whatever size or color beads you have.

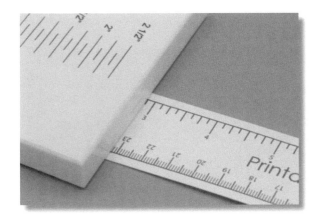

With this necklace we will be creating an 8"
measurement between the crystal and knot. This is
where we are going to be using the ruler. I printed a
ruler from printable-ruler.net from the Internet. I cut
it to size and taped it to the back of my Easy
Knotter. I started the ruler at the end of the Easy
Knotter at the 2 7/8" since that is the distance
between the post and the end of the Easy Knotter.
Please refer to the picture.

To start the necklace, tie a knot at the end of the cord. String on one crimp bead and the spring ring and
bring it down to the end of the cord by the knot. Take the needle back through the crimp bead, securing
the spring ring. Crimp the crimp bead and trim the excess cord. We want a knot right up to the crimp
bead. Using the Easy Knotter instructions on page 5 create a knot right up to the crimp bead.

String on one crystal and bring that down to the knot. We want a knot right up to the crystal. Again, using
the Easy Knotter instructions, create a knot right up to the crystal.

Now we want to do the 8" spacing. Create the loop for the knot and place it on the post. Close up the
loop. We want the previous knot at the 8" mark on the ruler. Pull until the previous knot is at 8". Lift the
knot off the post and tug. Please refer to the picture below.

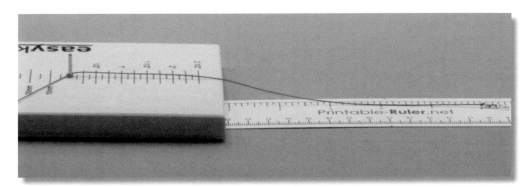

String on one seed bead, the
seven 3mm lapis beads and one
more seed bead. Bring the beads
down to the knot. We want a
knot right up to the seed bead.
Using the Easy Knotter
instructions on page 4 create a
knot right up to the seed bead.
Please refer to the picture.

Now we want another 8" spacing. Create the loop of the knot, place it on the post. Pull until the previous knot is at the 8". Lift the knot off the post and tug. Please refer to the picture below.

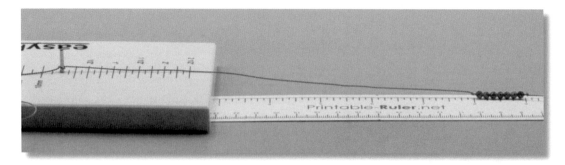

String one crystal and bring that down to the knot. We want a knot right up to the crystal. Using the Easy Knotter instructions, tie a knot right up to the crystal.

String on one crimp bead and one closed jump ring and bring the crimp bead and jump ring to the knot. Bring the needle back through the crimp bead securing the closed jump ring. Crimp the crimp bead making sure the crimp bead is right up to the last knot. Trim the excess cord and attach the crimp covers.

Enjoy!

PROJECT 2 – RICE AND COIN PEARL NECKLACE – 32"

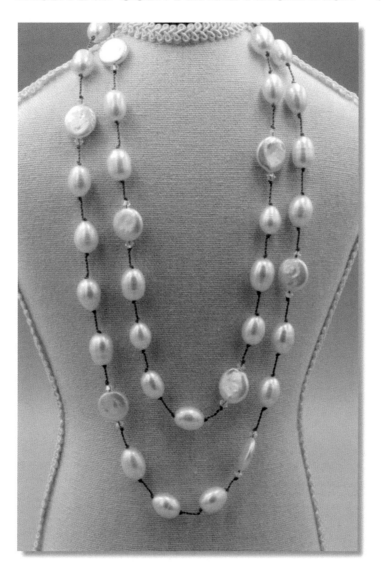

SUPPLIES NEEDED   -   Griffin Nylon Cord, Size 5, Beige
                                      29 – 12mm rice pearls
                                      10 – 12mm coin pearls
                                      20 – 2.5mm Swarovski bicone crystals
                                      2 – Crimping End Caps
                                      2 – 4mm open jump rings
                                      1 – toggle clasp

Whenever I want to dress up I reach for this necklace. Whether I'm wearing jeans and a tee shirt or my favorite outfit, this necklace always makes me feel good. Perfect length with just a sprinkle of Swarovski crystals. This necklace also looks good with smaller pearls. Just make sure the rice pearls and coin pearls are the same size.

To start the necklace, tie a knot at the end of the cord. String on one crimping end cap and bring it down to the knot. Create a loop for the knot, place the loop on the post 1 ½" away from the first knot. Lift the knot off the post. The crimping end cap will be floating between the knots. We will crimp the crimping end cap when we finish the necklace. This way, if a mistake is made or you don't like how it is coming out, you will not waste the crimping end cap.

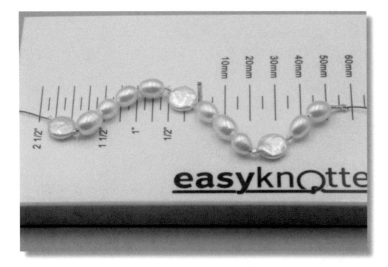

String on the beads in this order --- 2 rice pearls ---one crystal, one coin pearl, one crystal --- 3 rice pearls --- one crystal, one coin pearl, one crystal --- 4 rice pearls --- one crystal, one coin pearl, one crystal. Please see picture for reference. Repeat the above order of beads 2 more times. There will be three sets of the above pattern.

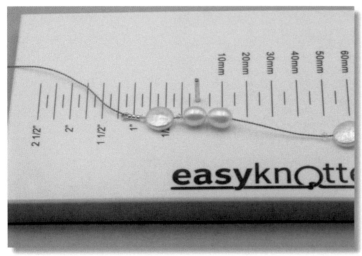

String on 2 more rice pearls and one crystal, one coin pearl, one crystal. Please refer to the picture. String on one crimping end cap.

Now to start knotting. With this necklace we will be using the ¼" spacing. Create the loop for the knot, place the loop on the post and using the Easy Knotter instructions on page 4 create the ¼" spacing. Lift the knot off the post and give a tug.

Bring down one rice pearl to the knot you just created. We want to create a knot right up to the rice pearl. Using the Easy Knotter instructions on page 5 create a knot right up to the rice pearl.

Continue with another ¼" spacing. Bring down the rice pearl to the knot and using the instructions above create a knot right up to the rice pearl. Continue again with another ¼" spacing.

Bring down one crystal, one coin pearl, one crystal to the knot. Create the loop for the knot, place the loop on the post and using the Easy Knotter instructions on page 5 create a knot right up to the crystal.

Using the instructions above continue knotting until all the beads are knotted.

Create one last ¼" measurement. Put a little bit of glue above the last knot. Bring down the crimping end cap to the knot. Crimp the crimping end cap. Repeat on the opposite side. Trim the excess cord and attach the toggle with the open jump rings.

Enjoy!!

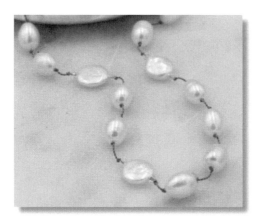

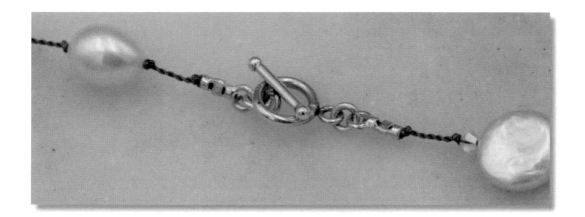

PROJECT 3 – LABRADORITE, CRYSTALS AND CHAIN NECKLACE – 34"

SUPPLIES NEEDED   -   Griffin nylon cord, size 6, gray
24 – 12x18mm oval labradorite beads
48 – 2.5mm Swarovski bicone crystals
24" of 6.2mm oval chain
6" of 6.2mm oval chain
5" of 6.2mm oval chain
4" of 6.2mm oval chain
2 – 4mm open jump rings
3 – 2" headpins
2 – 2x3mm crimp beads
2 – 3mm crimp covers
1 – toggle clasp

I was having so much fun with this necklace. You can wear it so many different ways. Wear the chain in the front, have the chain down your back or even wear it on the side in the front. It looks great any way you wear it. The labradorite beads are just beautiful. I found them at Stone USA in New York City.

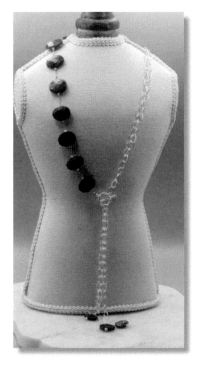

To start the necklace, tie a knot at the end of the cord and bring the crimp bead down to the end of the cord. Bring down the circle part of the toggle next to the crimp bead. Bring the needle back through the crimp bead and pull until the crimp bead is up to the toggle. Crimp the crimp bead and trim the excess cord. We want a knot next to the crimp bead. Create the loop for the knot and using the Easy Knotter instructions on page 5 create the knot right up to the crimp bead.

String the beads on in this order --- one crystal, one labradorite bead, one crystal. Continue this pattern until you have 21 labradorite beads and 42 crystals on the cord.

Now to start knotting. Bring down one crystal, one labradorite bead and one crystal to the knot you just created. We want to create a knot right up to the crystal. Create a loop for the knot, place the loop on the post and using the Easy Knotter instructions on page 5 create a knot right up to the crystal.

With this necklace we will be using the ¼" spacing. Create the loop for the knot, place the loop on the post and using the Easy Knotter instructions on page 4 create the ¼" spacing. Lift the knot off the post and give a tug.

Bring down one crystal, one labradorite bead, one crystal to the knot. Using the instructions above, create a knot right up to the crystal.

Create another 1/4" measurement and continue the pattern above until all the beads are knotted.

After you finished knotting, string on the crimp bead to the knot. Find the center of the 24 inch chain and string the chain next to the crimp bead. Bring the needle back through the crimp bead and pull until the crimp bead is next to the chain. Crimp the crimp bead making sure the crimp bead is by the knot. Please refer to the picture.

Trim the excess cord, attach the other part of the toggle to the two chain ends with the jump ring. Please refer to the picture.

Using the instructions on wire wrapping on page 10, wire wrap the crystal, labradorite bead, crystal on the six, five and four inch chain. When you create the loop for the wire wrap, attach the chain within the loop. Please refer to the picture.

 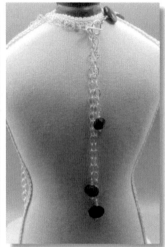

Attach the chains with the wire wrap and the circle part of the toggle to the open jump ring. Close up the jump ring!

Enjoy!

PROJECT 4 – TRIPLE STRAND CZECH BEAD AND CRYSTAL BRACELET – 6" WITH 2" EXTENDER CHAIN

SUPPLIES NEEDED   -   Griffin nylon cord, size 6, gray
22 – 8mm rondelle shape Czech beads
43 – 2.5mm Swarovski bicone crystals AB
6 – 2x3mm crimp beads
6 – 3mm crimp covers
2 – triple strand ends
1 – 4mm open jump ring
1 – 9mm lobster clasp
1 – 2" 4mm chain
1 – 2" head pin

I was attending Beadfest over in Oaks, PA a few months ago. It felt really strange being there as a customer and not a vendor. Since my Easy Knotter is now licensed to Beadsmith, we no longer are a vendor at the trade shows. I was loving every minute of Beadfest. I usually do a walk through first and them go back to what I want to purchase, even though I don't need any more beads. But then again, you can never have too many beads. I walked past the booth – Nirvana Beads, exceptional Czech glass for artists and this strand that looks like an incredible sunset caught my eye. Beautiful. I walked

away and after a few steps I knew I had to have them. I love working with the Czech glass. So much you can do with them. Any beads that you use for this bracelet will look beautiful!

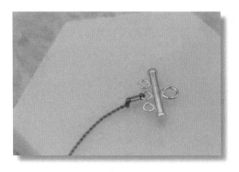

To start the bracelet, tie a knot at the end of the cord. String on one crimp bead and bring it down to the knot. Take the needle and thread it through the middle hole of the triple strand end. I like to start in the middle of the triple strand end. It makes it easier to crimp the crimp bead. Bring the triple strand end to the crimp bead. Take the needle back through the crimp bead securing the triple end strand. Crimp the crimp bead and trim the excess cord. Please refer to the picture.

We want a knot right up to the crimp bead. Create the loop for the knot and place it on the post. Using the Easy Knotter instructions on page 5 create a knot right up to the crimp bead.

String the beads on in this order. One crystal, one Czech bead, one crystal. Repeat this pattern until you have seven sets on the cord. Bring down one crystal, one Czech bead and one crystal to the knot. We want a knot right up to the crystal. Using the Easy Knotter instructions on page 5 create a knot right up to the crystal.

For this bracelet we will be using the ¼" measurement. Create the loop for the knot and place it on the post. Using the Easy Knotter instructions on page 4 create the ¼" measurement. Lift the knot off the post and give a tug.

Using the pattern above, continue knotting until all the seven sets of beads are knotted. End with a ¼" measurement. Please refer to the picture.

String on one crimp bead and bring it to the knot. Take the needle and thread it through the middle hole of the second triple strand end. Bring the triple strand end to the crimp bread. Crimp the crimp bead next to the knot and trim the excess cord. Please see picture.

Attach the crimp cover to the crimp beads.

Now to start the outside strand. We are going to start on the triple strand end side you just finished with the ¼" measurement. This way the beads will be staggered. Tie a knot at the end of the cord and string on one crimp bead to the knot. Take the needle and thread it through the outside strand of the triple strand end. Bring the needle back through the crimp bead securing the triple strand end. Crimp the crimp bead and trim the excess cord.

String on seven sets of one crystal, one Czech bead, one crystal. Using the instructions above, knot the end strand starting with a knot by the crimp bead and then bring down one crystal, one Czech bead, one crystal and knot. Continue with the ¼" measurement. Please refer to the picture.

When you have knotted all seven sets of the beads, end with one last ¼" measurement.

String on one crimp bead and bring it to the knot. Take the needle and thread it through the end hole of the second triple strand end. Bring the triple strand end to the crimp bread. Crimp the crimp bead and trim the excess cord. Please refer to the picture.

Attach the crimp cover to the crimp beads.

Using the instructions above for the outside strand, repeat this for the opposite outside strand. Again, start this strand by the ¼" measurement of the middle strand. Please refer to the picture.

Place the crystal and Czech bead on the head pin. Using the wire wrapping instructions on page 10 wire wrap the crystal and Czech bead. When you create the loop for the wire wrap, attach the chain within the loop. Please refer to the picture.

Attach the chain to the triple strand end with a jump ring and attach the lobster clasp on the opposite side.

Enjoy!

PROJECT 5 – CUBIC ZIRCONIA FLOATER NECKLACE – 38"

SUPPLIES NEEDED   -   2 – Griffin nylon cord, size 3, beige
94 – 8mm heart shaped cubic zirconia beads
2 – crimping end caps
1 – 5mm open jump ring
1 – 9mm lobster clasp

I have always had a passion for cubic zirconia. The colors are stunning. The facets on the heart shaped cubic zirconia is absolutely beautiful. I found the cubic zirconia beads at Stone USA in New York City. I can spend hours at the bead store. One thing I want to mention when you create this necklace, make sure you have enough room to work. You will be working with thin cords and the cords can get tangled. This necklace also looks beautiful with heart shaped glass beads or teardrop glass beads.

To start the necklace, open up both cords. Bring both ends together and tie a knot at the end of the cords. String on one crimping end cap to both cords and bring it down to the knot. Create a loop for the knot, place the knot on the post 1 ½" away from the first knot. Lift the knot off the post. The crimping end cap will be floating between the knots. We will crimp the crimping end cap when we finish the necklace. This way, if a mistake is made or you don't like how it is coming out, you will not waste the crimping end cap.

We are using 94 cubic zirconia beads. 47 beads will be on one cord and 47 on the other cord. What I like to do is put the dark beads on one cord and the lighter beads on the other cord. Please refer to the picture below. Since we are using a thin cord, I want to stress that you need enough room to work. You don't want to get the cords tangled.

To start knotting, bring two cubic zirconia beads down to the knot, one from each cord making sure the two cords are separated while bringing the beads to the knot. Please refer to the picture.

There will be two beads by the knot. For this necklace we are using the ¾" measurement. Bring the two cords together and using the Easy Knotter instructions on page 4 create the ¾" measurement making sure both cords are even. The cubic zirconia's will be floating between the knots. Please refer to the picture.

Continue the instruction above bringing two cubic zirconia beads down to the knot, one from each cord, until all the cubic zirconia beads are knotted.

To finish the necklace, put a little bit of glue above the last knot. Bring down the crimping end cap to the knot. Crimp the crimping end cap. Repeat on the opposite side. Trim the excess cord and attach the lobster clasp on one side and the jump ring on the opposite side.

Enjoy!

PROJECT 6 – PENDANT NECKLACE – 17" WITH ADDITIONAL 7" FOR PENDANT

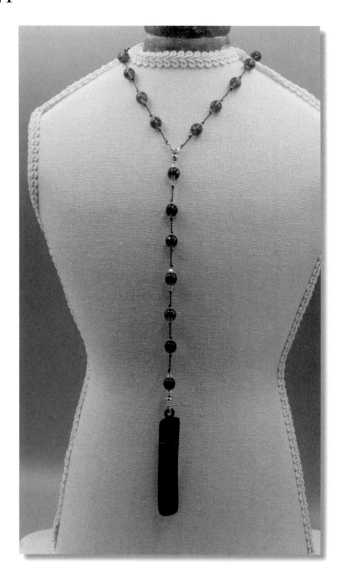

SUPPLIES NEEDED   -

Griffin nylon cord, size 4, brown
33 – 6mm faceted smokey quartz
80 – gold plated metal seed bead, size 15
8 – 2.5mm Swarovski bicone crystal AB
1 – pendant of your choice
1 – 3mm sterling silver closed jump ring
4 – 2x3mm crimp bead
4 – 3mm gold plated crimp cover
1 – 5mm gold plated closed jump ring
1 – 5mm gold plated spring ring

I was searching on Etsy for a rustic Celtic cross and came across this pendant. I love the simplicity of it. Goes perfectly with the smokey quartz and gold seed beads. It's a beautiful necklace for any outfit. I am using the gold seed beads throughout this necklace. I love the look and also it helps keep the bead in place. The hole of the 6mm smokey quartz bead is too large for the knot. I wanted to use the thinner cord and by using the gold seed beads to hold the smokey quartz in place, it's perfect.

We will start the necklace creating the pendant first. Tie a knot at the end of the cord. String on one crimp bead and the 3mm silver closed jump ring and bring it down to the end of the cord by the knot. Take the needle back through the crimp bead, securing the jump ring. Crimp the crimp bead and trim the excess cord. We want a knot right up to the crimp bead. Using the Easy Knotter instructions on page 5 create a knot right up to the crimp bead.

String on the beads in this order – one seed bead, one crystal, one smokey quartz bead, one crystal, one seed bead --- TWO sets of one seed bead, one smokey quartz bead, one seed bead --- REPEAT THE ABOVE PATTERN ONCE MORE --- end with one more seed bead, one crystal, one smokey quartz bead, one crystal, one seed bead.

Now to start knotting. Bring down one gold seed bead, one crystal, one smokey quartz bead, one crystal and one gold seed bead to the knot. Using the Easy Knotter instructions on page 5 we want to create a knot right up to the gold seed bead.

For this necklace we are using the ¼" measurement. Using the Easy Knotter instructions on page 4 create a ¼" spacing.

Bring down one seed bead, one smokey quartz, one seed bead to the knot. Using the Easy Knotter instructions on page 5 create a knot right up to the seed bead.

Using the pattern above, continue knotting starting with another ¼" measurement until all the beads are knotted.

String on one crimp bead --- ten gold seed beads and the pendant and bring this down to the knot. Bring the needle back through the crimp bead and pull until you secure the seed beads and pendant. The pendant will be floating on the seed beads. Please refer to the picture.

Crimp the crimp bead by the knot. Trim the excess cord and attach the gold crimp covers.

Now to start the necklace. With the excess cord, tie a knot at the end of the cord. String on one crimp bead and the spring ring and bring it down to the end of the cord by the knot. Take the needle back through the crimp bead, securing the spring ring. Crimp the crimp bead and trim the excess cord. We want a knot right up to the crimp bead. Using the Easy Knotter instructions on page 5 create a knot right up to the crimp bead.

String on the beads in this order --- We want 13 sets of --- one seed bead, one smokey quartz, one seed bead --- after the 13 sets, string on one seed bead, one crystal, one seed bead, the pendant you just created, one seed bead, one crystal, one seed bead --- String on another 13 sets of --- one seed bead, one smokey quartz, one seed bead.

Now to start knotting. Bring down one seed bead, one smokey quartz, one seed bead to the knot. Using the Easy Knotter instructions on page 5 create a knot right up to the gold seed bead.

For this necklace we are using the ¼" measurement. Using the Easy Knotter instructions on page 4 create the ¼" measurement.

Using the instructions above, continue knotting the first 13 sets of one seed bead, one smokey quartz and one seed bead. After the last set, create another ¼" measurement.

For the pendant, bring down one seed bead, one crystal, one seed bead, the pendant, one seed bead, one crystal, one seed bead. Using the Easy Knotter instructions on page 5 we want a knot right up to the seed bead. Please refer to the picture.

Continue with another ¼" measurement and continue knotting the remaining 13 sets of beads with the ¼" measurements between the sets of beads. After the last knot by the seed bead, string on one crimp bead and one closed jump ring and bring the crimp bead and closed jump ring to the knot. Bring the needle back through the crimp bead securing the closed jump ring. Crimp the crimp bead making sure the crimp bead is right up to the last knot. Trim the excess cord and attach the crimp covers.

Enjoy!

PROJECT 7 – LARIAT NUMBER ONE – PEARLS AND CRYSTALS – 36"

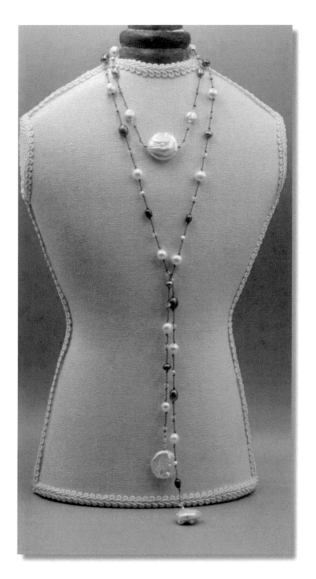

SUPPLIES NEEDED   -   Griffin nylon cord, size 6, beige
15 – assorted 3mm to 4mm pearls
14 – 6mm round white pearls
2 – 6mm white coin pearls
3 – 18mm white coin pearls
39 – 2.5mm Swarovski bicone crystals AB
4 – gold plated metal seed beads, size 11
10 – gold plated metal seed beads, size 15
2 – 2" sterling silver head pins
2 – 2x3mm crimp beads
2 – 3mm crimp covers

I love creating lariats. So simple and can be worn so many different ways. The way I design the lariats is having a center bead that complements the rest of the lariat. With this lariat it is the 18mm coin pearl. If you wear the lariat long, the coin pearl will be shown at the back of your neck. If you wear it doubled, the coin pearl will be shown right at the center of your neck. It all looks beautiful. You can also wear it as a bracelet!

To start, we will wire wrap the dangles for the lariat. With the head pin, string on one gold seed bead, size 15, one 18mm coin pearl, one gold seed bead, size 11, one 2.5mm crystal, one gold seed bead, size 15. Repeat with the other head pin. Using the wire wrapping instructions on page 10 wire wrap the dangles for the lariat.

With the cord, tie a knot at the end of the cord. String on one crimp bead and one wire wrapped dangle and bring the crimp bead and dangle to the knot. Bring the needle back through the crimp bead securing the dangle. Crimp the crimp bead. Trim the excess cord and attach the crimp cover. Please refer to the picture.

We want a knot right up to the crimp bead. Using the Easy Knotter instructions on page 5 create a knot right up to the crimp bead.

String the beads on in this order --- one crystal – one 6mm white pearl – one crystal – one of the assorted pearls --- Repeat this pattern six more times – there will be seven sets of the above beads.

For the center of the lariat, string the beads on in this order --- one crystal -- one gold seed bead, size 15, one crystal, one 6mm coin pearl, one crystal, one gold seed bead, size 15 --- one gold seed bead, size 15, one crystal, one gold seed bead, size 11, one 18mm coin pearl, one gold seed bead, size 11, one crystal, one gold seed bead, size 15 --- one gold seed bead, size 15, one crystal, one 6mm coin pearl, one crystal, one gold seed bead, size 15 --- one crystal.

Continue stringing the beads on in this order --- one assorted pearl, one crystal, one 6mm white pearl, one crystal --- Repeat this pattern six more times – there will be seven sets of the above beads.

We want to add one more assorted pearl and one more crystal. With the lariats I like to have one side just a little bit longer, this way it will give the lariat more character with the dangles staggered. The two extra beads will give it the extra spacing so the dangles will not be even.

Now to start knotting. Bring down one crystal to the knot. Using the Easy Knotter instructions on page 5 we want a knot right up to the crystal.

For this lariat we will be using the ¼" measurement. Using the Easy Knotter instructions on page 4 create a ¼" measurement.

Bring down one pearl to the knot. Using the Easy Knotter instructions on page 5 we want a knot right up to the pearl. Please refer to the picture.

Continue knotting until you get to the center of the lariat. Bring down one crystal to the knot and knot right up to the crystal. Create a ¼" measurement. Bring down the seed bead, crystal, 6mm coin pearl, crystal, seed bead to the knot and knot right up to the seed bead. Create another ¼" measurement. Bring down one seed bead, size 15, one crystal, one seed bead, size 11, 18mm coin pearl, one seed bead, size 11, one crystal, one seed bead, size 15 to the knot and knot right up to the seed bead. Create another ¼" measurement. Bring down one seed bead, one crystal, one 6mm coin pearl, one crystal, one seed bead to the knot and knot right up to the seed bead. Create another ¼" measurement and bring one crystal down to the knot. Create a knot right up to the crystal. Please refer to the picture.

Create another ¼" measurement. Bring one assorted pearl to the knot and knot right up to the pearl. Continue knotting the rest of the beads with the ¼" measurement between the beads.

After the last knotted crystal, string on one crimp bead and the dangle and bring this to the knot. Bring the needle back through the crimp bead securing the dangle. Crimp the crimp bead making sure the crimp bead is right up to the knot. Trim the excess cord and attach the crimp covers.

Enjoy!

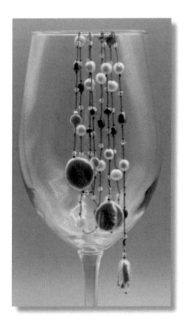

PROJECT 8 – LARIAT NUMBER TWO – PEARLS, TURQUOISE PENDANT, CRYSTALS AND BEADS – 42"

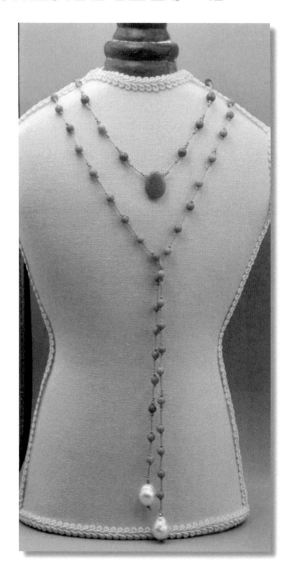

SUPPLIES NEEDED   -   Griffin silk cord, size 6, amber
2 – 12mm Baroque pearls
48 – 4mm turquoise color beads
8 – 4mm coral beads
40 – 2.5mm Swarovski bicone crystals, light topaz AB
6 – 4mm Swarovski bicone crystal, topaz AB
52 – gold plated metal seed beads, size 15
1 – 14mm turquoise teardrop pendant or pendant of our choice

I decided to add another lariat to the book. I wanted to show you different color combinations and how you can change the center bead for a different look. Also, there is no wire wrapping for the dangles. We are just going to add a little glue to the ending knots. There are no findings with this lariat. I always imagine myself sitting on a beach watching the waves and creating lariats. So calming, so peaceful!

To start the lariat, tie a knot at the end of the cord and place the beads on in this order. One baroque pearl, one crystal, one seed bead.

String on four turquoise color beads --- one seed bead, one 2.5mm crystal, one turquoise color bead, one 2.5mm crystal, one seed bead --- repeat this pattern three more times. There will be 4 sets of the above beads.

String on four more turquoise color beads.

String on one seed bead, one 4mm crystal, one seed bead --- one seed bead, one 2.5mm crystal, one coral bead, one 2.5mm crystal, one seed bead --- Repeat this pattern two more times. There will be 3 sets of the above beads.

String on one seed bead, one 2.5mm crystal, one turquoise color bead, one 2.5mm crystal, one seed bead --- one seed bead, one 2.5mm crystal, one coral bead, one 2.5mm crystal, one seed bead – one seed bead, one 2.5mm crystal, turquoise pendant, one 2.5mm crystal, one seed bead.

We are going to string the beads on the opposite side of the lariat in reverse order. String on one seed bead, one 2.5mm crystal, one coral bead, one 2.5mm crystal, one seed bead --- one seed bead, one 2.5mm crystal, one turquoise color bead, one 2.5mm crystal, one seed bead.

String on one seed bead, one 2.5mm crystal, one coral bead, one 2.5mm crystal, one seed bead --- one seed bead, one 4mm crystal, one seed bead. Repeat this pattern two more times. You will have 3 sets of the above beads.

String on four turquoise color beads --- one seed bead, one 2.5mm crystal, one turquoise color bead, one 2.5mm crystal, one seed bead --- repeat this pattern three more times. There will be 4 sets of the above beads. String on two additional turquoise color beads. The two extra beads will give the lariat more character with one end of the lariat longer than the other end.

String on one seed bead, one 2.5mm crystal and the baroque pearl.

Now to start knotting. Bring the baroque pearl, crystal and seed bead to the knot. We want a knot right up to the seed bead. Using the Easy Knotter instructions on page 5 create a knot right up to the seed bead.

For this lariat we are using the ¼" measurement. Using the Easy Knotter instructions on page 4 create a ¼" measurement.

Bring down one turquoise color bead to the knot. Using the Easy Knotter instructions on page 4 we want a knot right up to the bead. Continue knotting the turquoise color beads with ¼" measurement between the beads. Bring down the set of beads to the knot – one seed bead, one crystal, one turquoise color bead, one crystal one seed bead and knot right up to the seed bead. Please refer to the picture.

Continue knotting the four sets of the turquoise color beads with ¼" measurements between the beads.

For the center part of the lariat you will be bringing the beads down to the knot in sets with ¼" measurement between the sets. Bring down one seed bead, one crystal, and one seed bead to the knot and knot right up to the seed bead. Continue this pattern until all the sets are knotted. Please refer to the picture.

We are going to finish knotting the opposite side of the lariat using the same pattern above. Bring down one turquoise color bead to the knot. Using the Easy Knotter instructions on page 5 we want a knot right up to the bead. Continue knotting the turquoise color beads with ¼" measurement between the beads. Bring down the set of beads to the knot – one seed bead, one crystal, one turquoise color bead, one crystal, one seed bead and knot right up to the seed bead.

Continue knotting the four sets of the turquoise color beads with ¼" measurements between the beads.

Continue knotting the last two turquoise color beads and the last set of the baroque pearl. Tie a knot at the end of the cord. Apply glue to the knot and about ½" of the cord. Wait for the glue to dry and trim the excess cord. Please see pictures below.

Enjoy!

PROJECT 9 – 9 ½ feet MISCELLANEOUS OPAL BEADS WITH CRYSTALS AND TREATED PYRITE

SUPPLIES NEEDED   -   3 – Griffin nylon cord, size 6, beige
210 – 6mm rondelle assorted opals
39 – 5mm treated pyrite – gold color
78 – 2.5mm Swarovski bicone crystal AB
4 – 2x3mm crimp beads
4 – 3mm gold crimp covers
1 – 5mm gold closed jump ring
1 – 5mm gold closed spring ring

I had received many requests for one really long necklace. I came up with this one. With a longer necklace you want a cord that is at least a size 6, nothing thinner. If you used a thinner cord, the necklace would get tangled and you would get frustrated. You can wear this necklace so many different ways. Just keep wrapping around your neck. You can also wear I as a bracelet. It is one of those necklaces that people stop you on the street wanting to know where you got it. Use whatever beads you have. All will look beautiful!

For this necklace we will be doing it in stages. Three separate cords and then bringing all the cords together at the end. For this necklace we are just doing one knot. We will not be doing the knot of both sides of the bead. Gravity will bring the beads down to the knot.

For the first strand, tie a knot at the end of the cord. String on one crimp bead and the spring ring and bring it down to the end of the cord by the knot. Take the needle back through the crimp bead, securing the spring ring. Crimp the crimp bead and trim the excess cord. We want a knot right up to the crimp bead. Using the Easy Knotter instructions on page 5 create a knot right up to the crimp bead.

My strands of beads are assorted colors of opal, I picked the beads at random, any color combination will be beautiful.

String the beads on in this order, two opal beads --one crystal, one opal bead, one crystal --two more opal beads, one pyrite bead. Please refer to the picture.

Repeat this set of beads twelve more times with a total of 13 sets of beads. String on two more opal beads – one crystal, one opal bead, one crystal --two more opal beads. Once all the beads are on the cord, set it aside and start the second strand.

For the second strand, tie a knot at the end of the cord. String on one crimp bead and the jump ring and bring it down to the end of the cord by the knot. Take the needle back through the crimp bead, securing the jump ring. Crimp the crimp bead and trim the excess cord. We want a knot right up to the crimp bead. Using the Easy Knotter instructions on page 5 create a knot right up to the crimp bead.

We are going to string the beads on in the same order as the first strand. After the beads are on the cord, set it aside and start the third cord.

For the third cord, tie a double knot at the end of the cord. You want a large enough knot so the crimp bead does not fall off. You can also put a piece of tape by the knot to secure the crimp bead. String on one crimp bead. We are not crimping the crimp bead until after all the knotting is completed. String the beads on in the same order as the first and second strand.

Now to start knotting. Take the first stand and bring the opal bead to the knot by the crimp bead. Using the Easy Knotter instructions on page 5 create a knot right up to the opal bead. Bring down one opal bead to the knot. For this necklace we are going to be using the ¼" measurement, but instead of the previous knot at the ¼" measurement, the bead will be at the ¼" measurement. Using the Easy Knotter instructions on page 4 create a ¼" measurement.

Bring down another opal bead to the knot and create another ¼" measurement. Bring down one crystal, one opal bead, one crystal to the knot and create another ¼" measurement. Bring down one opal bead to the knot and create another ¼" measurement. Bring down one opal bead to the knot and create another ¼" measurement. Bring down one pyrite bead to the knot and create a ¼" measurement. Repeat the above pattern until all the beads are knotted ending with a ¼" measurement. Please see pictures below for placement of the beads. The beads are at the ¼" measurement, not the knot.

Repeat the above knotting for the second strand.

For the third strand, tie a knot about one inch from the crimp bead at the end of the cord. We will crimp the crimp bead after all strands are knotted. Knot this strand the same way you knotted the other two strands.

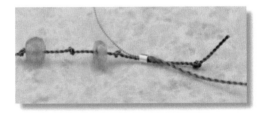

Now the fun begins, putting all three strands together. Take the first strand and third strand. With the needle of the first strand, bring it through the crimp bead of the third strand. Bring the cords together so the crimp bead is between the knots. Crimp the crimp bead and trim the excess cord. Please trim the right cord, not the knotted cord. Please refer to the pictures.

Take the second strand and third strand. String on one crimp bead on the third strand. We are using the same process of connecting the cords together as we did with the first strand. With the needle of the second strand, bring it through the crimp bead on the third strand. Bring the cords together so the crimp bead is between the knots. Crimp the crimp bead and trim the excess cord. Please trim the right cord, not the knotted cord.

To finish the necklace, attach the crimp covers.

Enjoy!

PROJECT 10 – MARQUISE SHAPE CHRYSOPHRASE
GRADUATED NECKLACE – 25"

SUPPLIES NEEDED -   12 feet of dark brown silk cord, size fff
1 – collapsible eye needle
1 – strand of graduated marquise shape chrysophrase 17x55mmm
20 – 8mm round chrysophrase beads
40 – 4mm Swarovski bicone crystal – light peach AB
40 – gold plated metal seed beads, size 15
2 – crimping end caps
2 – 5mm open jump ring
1 – toggle clasp

While shopping for beads at New York Jewelry Mart in New York City I came across this strand of graduated marquise shape chrysophrase. They were beautiful! The size of the beads are way out of my comfort zone. I like small and delicate beads but I knew I had to have them. I found round chrysophrase beads to go with this. If you want to get noticed, wear this necklace. It looks gorgeous with so many outfits.

Before we start the necklace, I want to talk about the graduated strand of chrysophrase. When creating a graduated strand, you want to have an uneven number of beads of the marquise shape. The largest bead will be in the center of the necklace and then gradually get smaller at the beginning of the necklace. My strand came with 20 beads. I used 19. I made sure the center bead was the largest and then gradually getting smaller to the beginning of the necklace. Please refer to the picture.

With the one extra left over bead I was able to make a necklace following the pattern for the minimalist necklace on page 13.

Working with large beads for this necklace, we are going to stretch the cord. Please refer to page 9 on how to stretch the cord.

To start the necklace, have your graduated beads on your mat the way you want to string them. With the cord, string on the collapsible eye needle and bring it to the center of the cord. Bring the two ends of the cord together and tie a knot. Please refer to the picture for the collapsible eye needle placement.

One more note about this necklace. We will be doing double knots for this project. The holes on the chrysophrase are quite large, and we need a large knot to keep it in place. I could not go to a larger cord since the crystals would not fit. To do a double knot, bring the cord through the loop twice. Knotting is the same technique as a single knot.

String on one crimping end cap and bring it down to the knot. Create a loop for the knot, bring the cord through the loop twice for a double knot. Place the knot on the post 1 ½" away from the first knot. Lift the knot off the post. The crimping end cap will be floating between the knots. We will crimp the crimping end cap when we finish the necklace. This way, if a mistake is made or you don't like how it is coming out, you will not waste the crimping end cap.

Put the beads on in this order. One crystal --- one seed bead, one round chrysophrase bead, one seed bead --- one crystal --- one marquise chrysophrase bead. Repeat this pattern until all the beads are on the cord.

Now to start knotting. Bring one crystal, one seed bead, one round chrysophrase bead, one seed bead and one crystal to the knot. Create the loop for the knot and bring the cord through twice (we are doing double knots) put the loop on the post. Using the Easy Knotter instructions on page 5 create a knot right up against the crystal. Bring down one marquise chrysophase bead to the knot. Create the double knot and put the loop on the post. Use the same method above to get the knot right up to the marquise chrysophase bead. Please refer to the picture.

Repeat this pattern until all the beads are knotted.

To end the necklace, string on the other crimping end cap. Put a little bit of glue above the last knot. Bring down the crimping end cap to the knot. Crimp the crimping end cap. Repeat on the opposite side. Trim the excess cord and attach the toggle with the open jump rings.

Enjoy!

PROJECT 11 – LEATHER BRACELET WITH WIRE WRAPPED BEADS – 14"

SUPPLIES NEEDED - 9 feet of 1mm leather
30 – 2" copper head pins
30 – 2.5mm Swarovski crystals AB
30 – assorted beads of your choice
2 – 10mm large hole pearl
1 – 4mm copper crimp cover

This was such a fun bracelet to put together. Just go through your bead stash, pick out your favorite beads and throw it all together. Any color combination and size of beads will look beautiful. I do recommend using a good quality leather. I used kangaroo leather. Hope you enjoy creating this bracelet.

Before we start the bracelet, wire wrap all the 30 beads. I put a crystal first and then the bead on the head pin and then wire wrapped. Please refer to page 10 on how to wire wrap.

Want to mention that when you wire wrap you want to make sure the loop of the wrap is large enough to go through your leather. What I do, I make a mark on my round-nose pliers on where to start my wire wrap (I used tape). This way all my wire wraps will be uniformed and will fit the cord. Please refer to the picture.

Now to start the bracelet. With one end of the leather fold over four inches. Bring the cords together so that there is a loop at the top. We want to create a ½" loop. The ½" loop is part of the clasp. Create a loop for the knot, place the loop of the knot on the post. Place the top loop of the leather at the ½" mark and pull until the knot is closed around the post. Take the knot off the post and give a tug. You will want to add a little glue to the knot. Please refer to the pictures below.

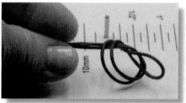

We are using the large hole pearl as our second part of the clasp at the end of the bracelet. Please make sure the pearl goes through the ½" loop you just created.

Take the 4mm copper crimp cover and put the two cords in the crimp cover by the knot you just created. Close up the crimp cover making sure both strands of leather are within the crimp cover. Trim the excess leather. Make sure you trim the right cord. Please refer to the picture.

For this bracelet we are using the ¼" measurement and our knots will be double knots. The double knot gives it a nice look.

To knot the leather you want to put the previous knot at your desired measurement and the loop on the post. Close up the loop. Doing it this way does not put extra stress on the leather cord by pulling it back and forth.

String on all wire wrapped beads in whatever way is pleasing to your eye. Bring down your first bead to the crimp cover. Create the loop for the knot and bring the leather through twice. Place the crimp cover at the ¼" measurement and the loop on the post. Pull the leather until the loop is closed on the post. With the double knot you want to make sure the two leather cords are right next to each other on the post. Take the knot off the post and give a tug. Please refer to the pictures.

Bring down your next wire wrapped bead and repeat the instructions above. Continue knotting until all the wire wrapped beads are knotted

To end the bracelet, create another ¼" measurement. We need this knot so there is space between the last wire wrapped bead and the large hole pearl. Please refer to the picture.

String on one large hole pearl and bring it down to the knot. Create the loop for the knot and bring the leather through the loop twice. Place the large hole pearl by the post. Place the loop on the post and pull until the loop is closed and the pearl is right up to the post. Take the second large hole pearl and string it on the leather. Push the large hole pearl to the knot on the post. Lift the knot off the post, push the large hole pearl to the knot to secure the knot of the first large hole pearl. Please refer to the pictures.

 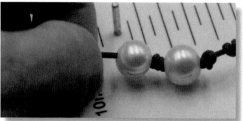

The second large hole pearl was the anchor bead. It helps to close up the knot. Remove the second large hole pearl from the leather. Add a little glue to the knot and trim the excess leather.

The knotted large hole pearl is the second part of the clasp. To close up the bracelet, wrap the bracelet around your wrist twice and push the large hole bead through the ½" loop at the beginning of the bracelet.

PROJECT 12 – TOURMALINE EARRINGS

SUPPLIES NEEDED   -   Griffin nylon cord, size 5, gray
12 – 6mm faceted coin tourmaline
24 – silver plated metal seed beads, size 15
2 – 3mm closed jump ring
2 – 2x3mm crimp beads
2 – 3mm crimp covers
1 pair of ear wires

I love making earrings. They are quick, easy and beautiful. Great way to use up leftover beads. I used tourmaline for the earrings. The facets on the tourmaline are gorgeous. Picked up this strand of tourmaline at Intrinsic Trading while I was at Beadfest in Oaks, PA. If you have never been to a bead trade show, I would highly recommend it. So much inspiration. Hope you have fun creating the earrings.

To start the earrings, tie a knot at the end of the cord. Arrange the beads on your mat the way you want to string them. String on one seed bead, one tourmaline bead, one seed bead. Repeat this two more times, with a total of three sets.

Bring down one seed bead, one tourmaline bead and one seed bead to the knot. We want a knot right up to the seed bead. Using the Easy Knotter instructions on page 5 create a knot right up to the seed bead.

For the earrings, we will be using the ¼" measurement. Using the Easy Knotter instructions on page 4 create the ¼" measurement.

Following the instructions above, bring down one seed bead, one tourmaline bead, one seed bead and knot right up to the seed bead.

Continue this pattern until you finished knotting.

Bring down one crimp bead and one closed jump ring to the knot. Take the needle back through the crimp bead securing the jump ring and crimp the crimp bead making sure the crimp bead is at the knot. Please refer to the picture.

To continue the earrings, string on one seed bead, one tourmaline bead, one seed bead. Repeat this two more times, with a total of three sets.

Now to start knotting the other side of the earring. We are going to start with a ¼" measurement. This way the earrings will be staggered. Please refer to picture.

Using the Easy Knotter instructions on page 4 create a ¼" measurement.

Bring down one seed bead, one tourmaline bead and one seed bead to the knot. We want a knot right up to the seed bead. Using the Easy Knotter instructions on page 5 create a knot right up to the seed bead. Please refer to the picture.

Next we want another ¼" measurement. Using the Easy Knotter instructions on page 4 create the ¼" measurement.

Following the instructions above, bring down one seed bead, one tourmaline bead, one seed bead and knot right up to the seed bead.

Continue this pattern until you finished knotting.

Once you have finished knotting, glue the knots at the end of the earrings. Wait for it to dry, trim the excess cord and attach the crimp cover.

Repeat the above process for the other earring. Attach earrings to earring wires.

Enjoy!

Thanks for reading! Again, I hope you enjoyed this book. I'm looking forward to writing the next one! One last thing: If you have trouble putting on clasped bracelets, try my other tool, the Bracelet Valet. Available at DesignsByReenie.com and my Etsy site, designsbyreenie., it makes this task a breeze! See below!

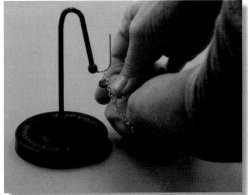

Made in the USA
Monee, IL
04 December 2020